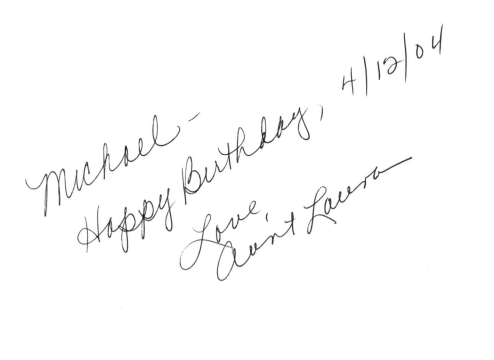

Michael –
Happy Birthday, 4/12/04
Love,
Aunt Laura

FASCINATING SCIENCE PROJECTS
ELECTRICITY
and MAGNETISM

Bobbi Searle

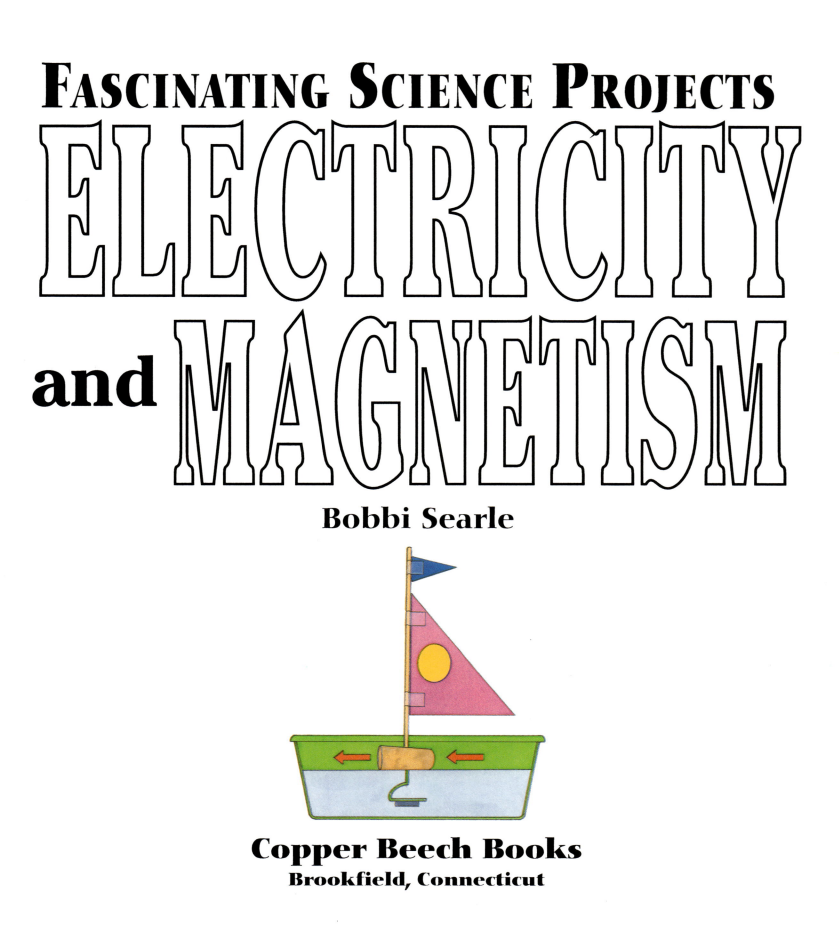

Copper Beech Books
Brookfield, Connecticut

© Aladdin Books Ltd 2002
Produced by
Aladdin Books Ltd
28 Percy Street
London W1T 2BZ

ISBN 0-7613-2715-0 (lib.bdg)
ISBN 0-7613-1630-2 (trade)

First published in the United States in 2002 by
Copper Beech Books,
an imprint of
The Millbrook Press
2 Old New Milford Road
Brookfield, Connecticut 06804

Designers:
Flick, Book Design and Graphics
Ian Thompson

Editor:
Harriet Brown

Illustrators:
Andrew Geeson, Catherine Ward,
and Peter Wilks—SGA
Cartoons:
Tony Kenyon—BL Kearley

Consultant:
Bryson Gore

Cataloging-in-Publication data is on file
at the Library of Congress.

Contents

Introduction

In this book, the science of electricity and magnetism is explained through a series of fascinating projects and experiments. Each chapter deals with a different topic on electricity and magnetism and contains a major project that is supported by simple experiments, "Magic panels," and "Fascinating fact" boxes. At the end of every chapter is an explanation of what has happened and what it means. Projects requiring sharp tools should be done under adult supervision.

This states the purpose of the project

METHOD NOTES
Helpful hints on things to remember when carrying out your project.

Materials
In this box is a full list of the items needed to carry out each main project.

1. The steps that describe how to carry out each project are listed clearly as numbered points.

2. Where there are illustrations to help you understand the instructions, the text refers to them as Figure 1, etc.

Figure 2

Figure 1

THE AMAZING MAGIC PANEL
This heading states what is happening

These boxes contain an activity or experiment that has a particularly dramatic or surprising result!

WHY IT WORKS
You can find out exactly what happened here, too.

WHY IT WORKS

These boxes, headed "Why it works," contain an explanation of what happened during your project, and the meaning of the result.

Fascinating facts!
An amusing or surprising fact related to the theme of the chapter.

Never use electricity with wet hands. Always make sure an adult knows what you are doing. If a project involves using a sharp knife, you will see this symbol. Always use insulated wire.

The text in these circles links the theme of the topic from one page to the next in the chapter.

What is electricity?

Electricity is a form of energy on which our daily lives depend. Many things in our homes and schools are powered by electricity. It provides energy in the form of heat to make light bulbs glow, and electrical impulses to make our computers work. Without it, our transportation systems would not work, and we wouldn't be able to communicate using telephones, e-mails, or text messages.

See how electricity can power a fan

METHOD NOTES
Hold your fan away from your face and eyes when you are using it.

Materials
- candy tube
- insulated wire
- transparent tape
- electric motor
- cardboard
- scissors
- battery

1. Take the lid off the candy tube and push the bottom out of the other end.
2. Cut two pieces of wire so that they are as long as the tube. Twist one end of each wire tightly onto each terminal at the back end of the motor (Figure 1).

Figure 1

6

Figure 2

Figure 3

3. Push the motor backward into one end of the tube (Figure 2).

4. Pull the wires through the tube and out the other end. Attach one end of each wire to a battery using transparent tape (Figure 3).

6. Cut out a small rectangle from some cardboard. Cut it in two places (Figure 4).

7. Bend one edge away from you and the other edge toward you to make a propeller shape (Figures 4 and 5).

8. Using a pencil, make a small hole in the middle of the propeller and push it onto the spindle of the motor.

9. Reattach the end of the wire to the battery. Tape the battery inside the tube and watch what happens to the propeller (Figure 6).

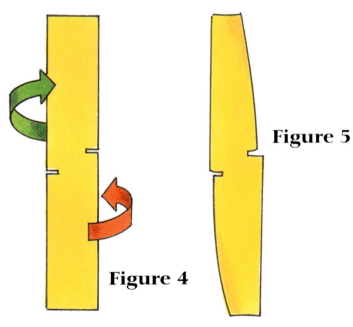

Figure 5

Figure 4

5. Take one wire off the battery to stop the motor until you need it.

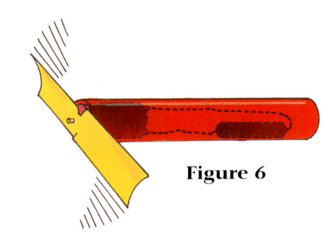

Figure 6

WHY IT WORKS

Electricity travels from the battery, through the wire, to the motor, and back to the battery. This is an electrical circuit. The electricity makes the motor spindle spin. By adding a propeller we can use electricity to spin it around and create wind.

What is electricity?

MAKE A SIMPLE SWITCH

1. Bend a long strip of copper into the shape shown (Figure 1) and glue it onto a piece of wood.
2. Glue a small piece of copper onto the edge of the wood, so that it hangs over the edge (Figure 1).
3. Glue a piece of cork to the top end of the long piece of copper (Figure 1).

Figure 1

Figure 2

5. Connect the other end of the wire to one side of a battery (Figure 2).
6. Attach a paper clip to the small piece of copper. Then attach a wire to the paper clip and to a small bulb. Attach a wire from the bulb to the battery (Figure 2).
7. Press the cork to touch the small piece of copper and watch the bulb light up.

4. Attach a paper clip to the long piece of copper at the end farthest from the cork, and attach a piece of wire to the paper clip.

Unbelievable speed!
If you turn on a switch, the electric signal travels at 186,000 miles per second (300,000 km/sec). That is as fast as the speed of light!

MAKE ANOTHER SWITCH

To make this simple circuit at right, begin by
pushing a thumbtack into some wood with
a paper clip under it. Connect the tack to a
bulb and the bulb to a battery, using insulated wire.
Connect the battery to a second thumbtack. Move the
loose end of the clip toward the tack and see the bulb light up.

MAKE A DIMMER SWITCH

Soak a pencil in water and then split it in
half down the middle (Figure 1). Glue it
onto a piece of wood and attach a wire to
each end of the pencil with crocodile clips.
Connect one of the wires to a battery.

Connect the second wire to a light bulb.
Attach another wire to the battery and to
the other side of the bulb. Gradually slide
one clip toward the other and watch the
bulb get brighter (Figure 2).

Figure 1

Figure 2

WHY IT WORKS

The graphite in the pencil is partially
resistant to electricity, so the electricity
finds it hard to go through. Therefore,
when you move the clips apart, the
light gets dimmer as the electricity has
to travel through more of the graphite.

Electricity
traveling around a circuit can be
stopped and started by a switch. Every
day we use hundreds of switches and
circuits to help us work, travel,
and prepare food.

Current

An electrical charge moving through a material is a current of electricity. For a current to flow there must be a circuit, or unbroken loop, for it to travel around. There must also be a force to push the charge along, from something like a battery. Current is a measure of the amount of electrical charge transferred from one place to another in a set amount of time.

See how current can make a motor spin

METHOD NOTES
Make sure your paper clips are long enough to hold the coil above the magnets.

Materials
- plastic cup
- 5 circular magnets
- 2 large paper clips
- insulated copper wire
- 4.5v battery
- a black marker pen

1. Wind the copper wire into a coil about 1 inch (2.5 cm) in diameter.
2. Wrap a short piece of wire once around the coil and leave 3/4 inch (2 cm) sticking out at each side.
3. Strip the ends off the copper wire and blacken the top half of one of the stripped wires using a marker (Figure 1).

Figure 1

4. Turn the cup upside down and place two magnets on top. Carefully place three more magnets inside the cup underneath the other magnets so they hold each other in place (Figure 2).

5. Unfold two paper clips and tape them to the sides of the cup (Figure 2).

Figure 2

6. Place the coil in between the paper clips and balance it above the magnets. Use the two wires sticking out (Figure 3) to keep it in place.

Figure 3

WHY IT WORKS

Electric current flowing through the wire coil causes one side of the coil to become a north pole and the other a south pole (see pages 30 to 33). The magnets on top of the cup repel and attract (or push and pull) the coil so that it spins around. Marking the wire black ensures that the current keeps the coil turning.

Figure 4

7. Attach two pieces of wire to the paper clips and then to a battery (Figure 4).

8. Give the coil a spin with your finger and watch what happens to your motor.

Current

Most substances allow electricity to flow through them, but not all do it well. How well something allows electricity to flow is measured by its resistance.

CONDUCTORS AND INSULATORS

Attach two wires to each end of a battery using transparent tape. Attach the other end of one wire to a bulb and the end of the other to a crocodile clip. Attach a third wire from the bulb to another crocodile clip (Figure 1). You have made a simple circuit with a gap in it so that you can add in different objects and test them.

Figure 1

WHY IT WORKS

If the object is a good conductor the light bulb will shine. A poor conductor (a resistor) will make the bulb shine dimly, and an insulator not at all.

Now attach the two crocodile clips to different objects (Figure 2). Some household objects are conductors, and some are insulators. Check the light bulb each time to see if electricity is flowing through the circuit.

Figure 2

Ouch, that hurts!
Did you know that the bite of a South American bushmaster snake can be treated by a series of electric shocks?

12

Figure 1

Figure 2

ELECTROPLATE A SPOON

Push two metal spoons through a piece of cardboard (Figure 1). Rest the cardboard across a bowl containing copper sulfate solution. Tape a wire to the end of each spoon. Attach the other ends of the wires to a battery, using paper clips (Figure 2). Watch what happens to the color of the spoons. Wash your hands thoroughly.

WHY IT WORKS

The electric current causes the copper in the solution to be attracted to the spoon connected to the negative battery terminal. The spoon becomes coated with copper. This works because the copper in the solution becomes positively charged.

MAKE A BATTERY TESTER

Wrap 6 feet (2 m) of insulated wire around a compass. Make sure you can still see north and south. Attach the two ends to a battery. The greater the current traveling through the wire, the more the compass needle will move. You can use this to test how much charge is in your batteries.

Current is the way electricity moves from one place to another. Different materials allow different amounts of electricity to go through them.

Batteries

Batteries are the most simple and convenient way of producing electricity. They contain stored chemical energy. The chemicals react with each other and produce an electrical charge. When the battery is connected in a circuit, this charge travels around the circuit as electrical current. Batteries come in all sizes—small ones in watches and large batteries to power cars.

Discover how a chemical reaction makes electricity

METHOD NOTES
Make sure you build your battery "cells" in the right order —coin, paper towel, then foil.

Materials

- lemon juice or salt
- 12 copper coins
- aluminum foil
- nail
- insulated wire
- a glass of water
- paper towel
- compass
- scissors
- teaspoon
- transparent tape

1. Draw around a coin and cut out 12 circles of foil (Figure 1).

2. Do the same with some paper towel.

3. Dissolve 10 teaspoons of salt in a glass of water (Figure 2) or add the juice of a lemon.

Figure 1

4. With your fingers carefully dampen the paper towel circles with the solution.

5. Make a tower by stacking the coins, paper towel, and foil on top of each other.

Figure 2

WHY IT WORKS

The coins react with the foil and the salt or lemon solution to produce electricity. When you attach the wires, the current is conducted from one metal coin to another through the salt water and foil. This current attracts the compass needle. Try removing the nail and bringing the ends of the wires together in a darkened room. You may see a little spark.

Figure 3

Figure 4

6. Wrap a wire tightly around a nail and attach the loose ends to the top and bottom of the pile with transparent tape (Figure 3).

7. Move the nail close to a compass and see how the needle moves (Figure 4). Make sure you wash your hands carefully.

How long?
Did you know that there is a battery that has been working since the year 1840?

Batteries
are one way of making electricity flow. They store energy and release it as electricity when we need to use it.

Batteries

MAKE A CHARGE CARRIER

Ask an adult to help you push a nail through the lid of a film canister. Wrap some foil around the bottom two-thirds of the canister and then fill it almost full with water. Put the lid on and make sure the nail is pushed down into the water (Figure 1). Rub a polystyrene tray with some yarn (Figure 2). Place an aluminum tray on top of it and touch the aluminum tray with your finger. There will be a spark.

Figure 1

Figure 2

Holding the canister by the foil, let the nail contact the aluminum tray (Figure 3). Don't touch the tray yourself. Now, touch the nail with your finger.

Figure 3

WHY IT WORKS

Rubbing the polystyrene tray makes it negatively charged. The aluminum tray sitting on the polystyrene one becomes negatively charged. Negative electrons jump onto you when you touch the aluminum tray. This leaves the tray positively charged and you negatively charged. Electrons move from the nail onto the positive tray. The nail is now positive. When you touch it, electrons are attracted from you into the nail. They are stored in the nail and in the water.

16

Don't breathe in the gas produced in this experiment.
Dissolve as much salt as you can in half a glass of water. Add some ink to the water, then pour it into a saucer. Attach two wires to a battery and dip the other ends into the water. Can you see the color of the ink disappear?

WHY IT WORKS

A chemical reaction produces bubbles of chlorine gas, which bleaches the ink and makes it disappear.

MAKE A WET BATTERY

Place a strip of zinc and a piece of copper pipe in a glass filled with white vinegar. Stick a piece of wire to each piece of metal.

Attach the other end of each wire to either side of a light-emitting diode (LED). The LED should glow red. If not, switch the wires on the LED. You could try using two pieces of zinc and copper. Metal plates in a liquid can cause a chemical reaction, which creates electricity to power your LED.

Some batteries, called primary batteries, must be thrown away once their chemicals have been used up. Others, such as car batteries, can be recharged and used again. They are called secondary batteries.

Static electricity

Some materials don't let electricity pass through them, but a static (still) electrical charge can be produced on their surface when they rub against certain other materials. This electrical charge can move when it is attracted by another charged object. When you take off your sweater, you might hear a crackling sound as you produce static electricity.

See how lightning can be made

METHOD NOTES
Do the last part of this experiment in a darkened room.

Materials
- a polystyrene tray
- an aluminum tray
- transparent tape
- scissors

1. Cut a corner off a polystyrene tray and stick it to the middle of an aluminum tray with transparent tape to make a handle (Figure 1).

Figure 1

Figure 2

2. Rub the bottom of the polystyrene tray on your hair really fast. Rub it from side to side (Figure 2)

3. Place the polystyrene tray upside down on a table.

Figure 3

4. Pick up the aluminum tray by the handle and carefully drop it onto the polystyrene tray (Figure 3). Don't touch the polystyrene tray!

5. While the aluminum tray is still on the polystyrene tray, touch the aluminum tray with your finger. Watch what happens.

6. Pick up the aluminum tray by the handle and touch it again with your finger (Figure 4). Can you see the lightning each time you touch the aluminum tray?

Figure 4

WHY IT WORKS

You create a negative charge on the polystyrene tray when you rub it on your hair. As you touch the aluminum tray, negative electrons leap to your hand. The second time, electrons jump from your hand to the positive tray and you see another spark.

19

Static electricity

Static electricity is a buildup of electrical charge. It can make objects attract or repel each other, and it can cause a spark.

MAKE AN ELECTROSCOPE

Cut two $1/2$ in (1 cm) by 2 in (4 cm) strips of aluminum foil (Figure 1). Open out a paper clip and push it through the center of a piece of cardboard. Hang the two pieces of foil on the hook of the paper clip (Figure 2). Place the cardboard over the top of a glass so that the foil and paper clip hang inside (Figure 3).

Figure 1

Figure 2

Figure 3

WHY IT WORKS

Bringing a charged object near the paper clip moves electrons out of the foil. Each foil strip then has the same charge so they repel each other and push apart.

Bring different charged objects, like combs or balloons that you have been rubbing on your hair, close to the paper clip. Watch what happens to the foil.

20

THE AMAZING BENDING WATER
Show how electrical charge attracts water

Comb your hair a few times with a plastic comb. Turn on the faucet and bring the comb close to the running water. Watch what happens to the flow of water.

WHY IT WORKS
The charged water coming from the faucet is attracted to the charged comb and moves toward it, making it bend!

STATIC ELECTRICITY NEWSPAPER

Cut a strip of newspaper 2 in (5 cm) by 12 in (30 cm). Put it on a table and stroke it 30 times with a cloth. Lower a plastic ruler and the paper will rise up to it.

Static electricity can be very powerful. The best example of this is lightning. Lightning contains a huge amount of electrical energy, which is changed into light, heat, and sound (thunder). The sparks caused by everyday static electricity are just small lightning bolts.

All around you

Have a look around you and count how many things you use every day that depend on electricity. Electricity is one of the easiest ways of producing light and heat in our world. Most electricity is produced by burning fossil fuels. Fossil fuels will not last forever, so scientists are finding ways of producing electricity using wind, solar, and water power. These sources are renewable.

Use electricity to make a secret room alarm

METHOD NOTES
When you have finished, hide your alarm under a rug or carpet so no one can see it.

Materials
- 4.5v battery
- transparent tape
- insulated wire
- stiff cardboard
- aluminum foil
- a light bulb

1. Fold a piece of cardboard in half.

2. Wrap a strip of foil around each side of the cardboard (Figure 1). Stick them in place with transparent tape.

Figure 1

6. Place the cardboard under a rug and hide the bulb so that only you can see it (Figure 3).

7. Watch what happens when the cardboard closes and the foil strips touch each other.

Figure 2

Figure 3

3. Tape a piece of wire to the foil on each side.

4. Connect the other end of one of the wires to a battery.

5. Attach the other wire to a bulb and then attach a third wire from the bulb to the battery (Figure 2).

WHY IT WORKS

When your intruder steps on the cardboard, the foil strips touch each other. This completes the electrical circuit, which allows the electrical current to flow and light the bulb.

So much electricity!
If everyone boiled only the water they needed, instead of filling the coffeemaker, we could save enough energy to light almost every street light in California!

Electricity heats metal objects to make them glow—this is how a light bulb produces light. You should always be careful not to touch metal that is connected in a circuit.

All around you

MAKE A MINER'S LIGHT

1. Cut a strip of cardboard long enough to fit around your head. Staple the two ends together (Figure 1).

2. Tape a small battery to the side of the headband.

3. Cut out a cardboard circle and carefully make a hole in the center.

Figure 1

4. Attach two long pieces of insulated wire to the back of a bulb (Figure 2).

5. Push the bulb and wires through the hole in the cardboard circle (Figure 3)

Figure 2

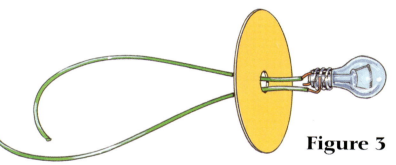

Figure 3

6. Tape the circle to the front of the headband.

7. Attach each wire to the battery at the side and tape the wires in place around the headband.

8. Your circuit is connected, and the bulb should now glow.

9. Place the miner's lamp on your head and try it out. See if it works for reading in bed.

Figure 4

THE AMAZING ELECTRICAL BALLOON
See a balloon light a fluorescent bulb

Ask an adult to help you with this experiment. In a dark room, rub a balloon from side to side on your hair. Do this lots of times. Touch the balloon to the end of a fluorescent light bulb and watch what happens.

WHY IT WORKS
You should see small sparks, and the bulb should glow. Electrons move from the balloon to the bulb, causing small sparks inside the bulb.

Figure 1

Figure 2

STATIC ELECTRICITY BELL
Place two empty metal food cans on plastic trays (Figure 1). Tie a metal paper clip to some thread, and tie the thread around another plastic tray. Rest this across the cans. Rub a balloon on your hair. Hold it next to one of the cans (Figure 2).

Static electricity causes the paper clip to be attracted and repelled. It swings between the cans, hitting them like a bell.

In the future, fossil fuels will run out. This is why new sources for electricity are always being sought.

What is magnetism?

Magnetism is a force that causes attraction or repulsion between objects. Magnets always contain metal. The atoms in a magnetic material, like iron or steel, all point in the same direction. Magnetism is used in many everyday things, such as telephones and motors. It is even used to help ships find their way in stormy seas.

Make a magnetic boat to see how magnets work

METHOD NOTES
Make sure you use waterproof glue for this experiment.

Materials
- a bowl
- water
- cardboard
- a skewer
- a cork
- scissors
- a small magnet
- a paper clip
- waterproof glue
- a large strong magnet
- 2 doweling rods
- transparent tape

Figure 1

1. Cut some sail and flag shapes from cardboard and decorate them (Figure 1).
2. Tape the sails to a doweling rod to make a mast for your boat.

Figure 2

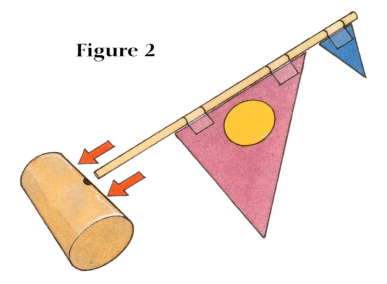

5. Unbend a paper clip as shown and glue a small magnet to the bottom of it (Figure 4).

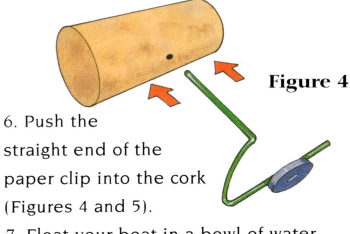

Figure 4

6. Push the straight end of the paper clip into the cork (Figures 4 and 5).

3. Make a small hole in the side of a cork with a skewer and push your mast into it (Figure 2).

4. Glue a large strong magnet to the end of the other doweling rod (Figure 3).

Figure 3

7. Float your boat in a bowl of water.

8. Use your magnet on the doweling rod to move your boat from underneath the bowl (Figure 5).

WHY IT WORKS

You can control the boat from underneath because the magnetic force travels through water. The two magnets attract or repel each other, depending which way up they are, causing your boat to move.

Figure 5

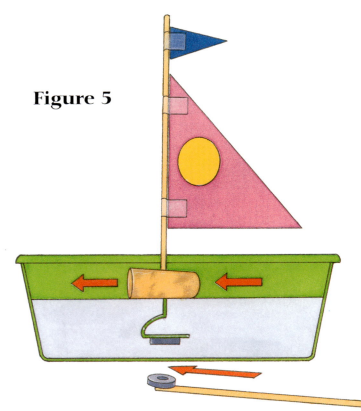

27

When the atoms of an object all point in different directions, the object is not magnetic. Some things, like plastic, wood, and some metals, can never be picked up with a magnet.

What is magnetism?

EXPERIMENT WITH MAGNETS

You can test the strength of a magnet by seeing how many paper clips or nails it can pick up. A strong magnet will pick up lots. Try experimenting with some household objects to see what else your magnet can pick up.

Try metal objects like keys, cutlery, and coins, and other objects made from wood, plastic, or rubber. Which ones can you pick up?

THE AMAZING DISAPPEARING SONG
See the effect of magnetism on recorded sound

Take an unwanted cassette and wind it back to the start. Unravel part of the tape. Wipe a magnet over it backward and forward several times. Wind the cassette back to the beginning and play it to see if the sound has changed.

WHY IT WORKS

The tape in cassettes is plastic tape with a coating of magnetic particles. These particles are in a regular pattern. Rubbing the magnet over the tape rearranges the particles and distorts or erases the recorded sound.

MAGNETIZE AND DEMAGNETIZE A NAIL

Take a large steel nail and bring a compass near it. Does the compass needle move? Point one end of the nail to north and place it on a piece of wood, or outside on the sidewalk. Put on a pair of safety goggles and hit the nail 50 times with a hammer (Figure 1).

Figure 1

Again, see what effect it has on a compass (Figure 2). Turn the nail around so it points south and hit it 50 more times. How does the needle move this time? Now line the nail up in an east–west direction and hit it 50 times more. Does the compass needle stay still this time?

WHY IT WORKS

When the nail is lined up with the north and south poles of the Earth and then hammered, it becomes magnetized. Hammering a nail like this makes the atoms point in the same direction. Hammering the nail when it is pointing east–west makes the atoms line up across the nail, and it appears demagnetized.

Figure 2

Magnetism is an invisible force, but we use its power everywhere we can. All electrical motors use it, and it is used for scientific research and to generate electricity.

Magnetic poles

Every magnet has two poles—north and south. If you broke a magnet into tiny pieces, each piece would still have a north and a south pole. The south pole of one magnet seeks the north pole of another magnet and repels the other's south pole. The Earth behaves like a giant magnet and has a magnetic north and south pole, which are close to the geographic North and South Poles.

See how magnets can show you the way

METHOD NOTES
Draw the compass points on the cardboard very carefully.

Materials
- a cup
- a needle
- a cork
- a protractor
- a magnet
- cardboard
- scissors
- water
- tape

1. Cut a circle from cardboard and then cut a hole in the center slightly smaller than the diameter of your cup (Figure 1).

Figure 1

2. Fill the cup with water almost to the top (Figure 2).

3. Make the needle magnetic by stroking it with one end of a magnet (Figure 3). Do this 30 times in the same direction.

4. Carefully cut a cork lengthwise and tape the needle to it (Figure 4).

5. Float the cork in the water with the needle facing upward.

6. Using a protractor, divide the circle into four equal parts and draw on the four compass points—north, south, east, and west (Figure 5).

Figure 2

Figure 3

Figure 4

Figure 5

7. Place the cardboard circle on top of the cup so the needle is pointing north to south (Figure 6).

8. Take your compass outside and try it.

WHY IT WORKS

Stroking a needle magnetizes it by lining up all the atoms in the same direction. The north-seeking pole of every magnet is always attracted to the magnetic north pole of the Earth. The north-seeking pole of a magnet is really its south pole as it is attracted to the magnetic north pole of Earth. As magnetic north is close to the geographic North Pole, this means you can always find out which way is north, south, east, and west.

Figure 6

Magnetic poles

There are two types of magnet—permanent and temporary. They both have a north and south pole. It is the pushing and pulling forces of magnets that make them so useful.

MAKE A COMPASS IN A GLASS

Place a needle on a table and stroke it in the same direction with one end of a magnet about 30 times (Figure 1). Fold a strip of cardboard in half and tape the magnetized needle to the inside. Fold the cardboard over the top (Figure 2). This is your compass strip.

Figure 1

Figure 2

Figure 3

Tie one end of a piece of string around the middle of the cardboard and tie the other end around the middle of a pencil. Place the pencil across the top of a glass.

The compass strip should hang inside the glass (Figure 3). Take your compass outside and watch the needle always point in the north–south direction.

Floating trains

Maglev trains don't have wheels. Instead, they float above the track because of magnetic repulsion between the tracks and the train. They can travel up to 300 mph (480 km/h)!

THE AMAZING FLOATING MAGNETS
Show the effect of magnetic levitation

Stick some modeling clay to a table. Push a piece of doweling into the clay. Make sure the doweling is just smaller in diameter than the center of the magnets. Put four or five doughnut magnets over the doweling. All the magnets must have their north poles facing other north poles.

WHY IT WORKS

When the magnets are placed north–north or south–south, they will "float" above each other. This is because similar poles repel each other.

INSECT WINDOW CLEANERS

Cut some insect shapes out of cardboard and decorate them. Glue a small magnet to the back of each one.

Glue a small piece of felt on top of the magnet. Place your insect on a window pane and hold it in place with another magnet on the other side. Move your insect around to clean the window. Only do this if you are on the first floor.

Opposite magnetic poles attract and similar poles repel. The south pole of a magnet is attracted to the north pole of the Earth. Compass needles work like this to help us find our way.

Magnetic fields

The area around a magnet is called the magnetic field. Magnetic fields are invisible, but we know that the field lines join the north end of the magnet to the south. A magnetic field is created by the magnetism of a permanent magnet or by an electric current. The larger the magnet and the closer an object is to the magnet, the greater the force of the magnetic field.

Discover what magnetic fields look like

METHOD NOTES
Make sure you take the label off the baby oil bottle before you start.

Materials
- a bottle of baby oil
- a magnet
- extra-fine steel wool
- scissors
- a teaspoon

1. Carefully open a bottle of baby oil.

2. Unroll the extra-fine steel wool and cut across it to get very short fibers. Cut a heaped teaspoonful (Figure 1).

Figure 1

3. Bunch the fibers together and drop them into the oil bottle (Figure 2).

4. Put the top on and shake the bottle by rotating it around and around. Don't shake it up and down.

Figure 2

5. Hold a strong magnet about an inch from the side of the bottle and watch what happens (Figure 3).

Figure 3

6. Don't hold it too close or all the fibers will clump together.

7. Try different ends of the magnet or more than one magnet to see what difference it makes to the pattern. Rotate the bottle each try.

You could also try this experiment with some short pieces of black hair cut from an old doll or party wig. Bring charged objects, like a balloon rubbed on your hair, toward the side of the bottle and see the patterns.

WHY IT WORKS

Iron filings align in strong magnetic fields so that all the north poles of the iron atoms point in the same direction. This reveals the shape of the three-dimensional magnetic field patterns. Small fibers of hair behave in a similar way when exposed to electric fields.

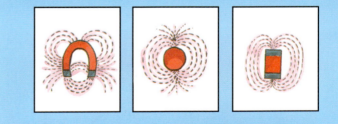

Charged balloons create electric fields by static electricity. The fibers begin to settle after 15 seconds so you need to keep rotating the bottle if you want to keep experimenting.

Invisible magnetic force fields are able to pass through some liquids and everyday objects made of glass and wood.

Magnetic fields

MAKE A MAGNETIC SHIELD

Glue two doweling rods along each side of a piece of cardboard. Glue another piece of cardboard on the doweling so there is a thin gap between the two pieces. Glue a strong magnet to the top edge of the cardboard. With the magnet end on top, let the shield hover above some paper clips. Does it pick them up?

WHY IT WORKS

When you insert the craft stick, the paper clips stay hanging, but when you insert the knife, they fall off. The magnetic field lines from the magnet pass through the craft stick, but the metal knife acts as a shield and stops the field lines from passing through.

Try putting a craft stick in the gap. Does it still attract the clips? Place a metal knife in between and watch what happens to the paper clips then.

Stormy weather

Did you know that the Earth experiences magnetic storms that can last for days at a time? The storms happen when electrically charged particles from the sun get trapped in the magnetic field of the Earth.

THE AMAZING JUMPING SNAKE
Show how electric current can create a magnetic field

Cut a stip of foil 15 in (40 cm) by 1/2 in (1 cm) and place it on a table. Put a horseshoe magnet across the strip. Attach two wires to a battery, and tape one end of one wire to one end of the strip. Quickly touch the other wire to the other end of the foil and watch the foil snake jump. Don't leave the battery connected for long and don't touch the foil—it could be hot.

WHY IT WORKS
An electric current flows through the foil and creates a magnetic field. This reacts with the magnetic field of the horseshoe magnet and causes the foil to be attracted and "jump" toward it.

MAKE A SWINGING MAGNET

Build a stand using three pieces of doweling. Push it into some modeling clay and place some round magnets underneath. They must all have the same pole facing up. Tie a magnet to some string and hang it from the stand. Swing it over the magnets and see how it reacts to the magnetic fields.

The magnetic fields of two or more magnets can react with each other to cause movement. Although magnetic fields are invisible, the movements they cause are fascinating to watch and experiment with.

Electromagnetism

An electromagnet is formed when a copper wire, connected to a battery, is coiled around a metal object like a nail. The electricity from the battery flows into the coil and produces a temporary magnetic field. Electromagnets come in all shapes and sizes. You use them in everyday items, such as doorbells and switches.

See how electricity magnetizes metal

METHOD NOTES
Make sure the ruler you use has a hole in the end of it.

Materials
- a horseshoe bolt
- insulated copper wire
- a long rubber band
- a long ruler
- string
- a jar or glass
- a battery
- two doweling rods
- transparent tape
- modeling clay
- a thread spool

1. Wrap some wire tightly around a horseshoe bolt, leaving the two long ends free (Figure 1).

Figure 1

2. Feed the two pieces of wire through the hole in the end of a ruler and tape them down the length of the ruler (Figure 2).

Figure 2

3. Attach the two wires to a battery.

4. Secure the ruler to the side of a glass or jar with a rubber band (Figure 3).

5. Lie the glass on its side and hold it in place with some modeling clay.

6. Tie a piece of string to the middle of the horseshoe bolt and feed it through the hole in the ruler so the bolt is dangling from the ruler (Figure 3).

Figure 3

7. Tape a piece of doweling to the ruler and push the spool onto one end (Figure 4).

Figure 4

8. Put a piece of doweling in the spool to act as a handle (Figure 4).

9. Tape the bolt's string to the spool and wrap the rest of the string around it.

10. Wind the magnet up and down to pick up objects (Figure 5).

Figure 5

WHY IT WORKS

The battery in your circuit sends an electric current into the wire around the metal bolt. This creates a magnetic field and turns the bolt into an electromagnet, or temporary magnet. Certain objects will be attracted to it so you can pick them up.

Electromagnetism

MAKE A RAILROAD SIGNAL

1. Wrap 6 ft (2 m) of wire around a straw, leaving 4 in (10 cm) free. Put a nail halfway into it (Figure 1).
2. Push a pushpin through another drinking straw, an inch (2 cm) from the top, into a piece of thick cardboard. Make sure the straw hangs loosely.
3. Cut out a signal arm shape from cardboard and make a small hole in the top (Figure 2).

Figure 1

4. Pin it to the cardboard near the top of the straw using a pushpin.
5. Wrap one end of a paper clip around the top of the straw and hook the other end through the signal arm (Figure 2).

Figure 2

WHY IT WORKS

When the battery is connected, the electric current flows through the wire coil and creates a magnetic field. The magnetized coil of wire attracts the nail inside the straw and pulls it to the left. This pulls the straw on the cardboard and moves the signal arm down.

6. Place the straw with the nail in it on the table so the head of the nail is hooked behind the straw (Figure 3).
7. Tape its wires to a battery and watch what happens to the signal arm (Figure 4).

Figure 3   **Figure 4**

THE AMAZING TALKING ELECTROMAGNET
See how radios collect signals from the air

Turn on a radio and tune it so it is between stations. Turn it up so there is a loud hissing noise. Hold an electromagnet close to the radio and listen as the sound changes when you connect the wires to the battery.

WHY IT WORKS
The electromagnet sends out electric current signals that the radio receives as clicking noises.

Figure 1

MAKE AN ELECTROMAGNET
Try experimenting with a simple electromagnet made from a nail, wire, and battery (Figure 1) and see how powerful it is.

See how many paper clips you can pick up at once. How does it compare to a permanent magnet? Try adding extra batteries to your circuit or extra wire to your nail and see what happens.

The strength of an electromagnet depends on the number of turns in the coil and the amount of the current traveling through the wire.

Amazing magnets

Magnets are incredibly versatile. They can be used as switches to turn machines on and off, as powerful cranes to lift heavy objects safely, or as simple refrigerator magnets to hold up your shopping list. The magnets in telephones, televisions, and radios even help change electrical impulses into sounds.

See how magnets are used in everyday life

METHOD NOTES
Make sure you fold the cardboard carefully to make the right shapes for the coin slots.

Materials
- a shoe box
- cardboard
- a magnet
- coins
- iron and steel washers
- transparent tape
- scissors

1. Cut a slot in one end of the shoe box. Make it about the length of a coin.

2. Cut a strip of cardboard and fold it into an "L" shape (Figure 1).

3. Cut another strip of cardboard and fold it 1 in (2.5 cm) from the top. Tape a magnet to the top of the cardboard (Figure 2).

Figure 1

Figure 2

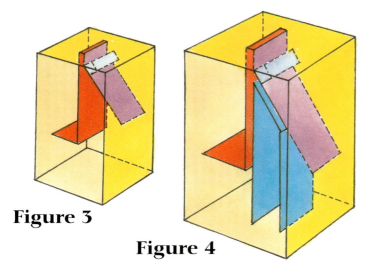

Figure 3

Figure 4

5. Tape the other cardboard with the magnet at the top, on the right of the slot (Figure 3).

6. Fold a third strip of cardboard to fit in the triangular space between the other two pieces of cardboard and tape it in place (Figure 4).

7. Drop your coins and washers down the slot and see which side they fall down(Figure 5).

4. Tape the "L"-shaped cardboard inside the box on the left of the slot.

WHY IT WORKS

Some coins are made from nonmagnetic metals. They are not attracted to the magnet and fall straight down. Iron and steel are magnetic metals and are attracted to the magnet. They fall down the right side of the box.

Figure 5

Magnetic creatures?
Did you know that some birds, insects, and fish have very small magnets in their bodies? Biologists think that these magnets help animals find their way when migrating.

Amazing magnets

Magnets are extremely good at finding metal hidden in other objects. In fact, a magnet could even find a needle in a haystack! You'd be surprised where metal can be found.

MAKE A SPINNING MAGNET

1. Mold some modeling clay and put it on a flat surface.

2. Carefully push the sharp end of a needle into the modeling clay (Figure 1).

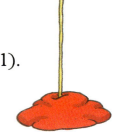

Figure 1

3. Place an aluminum cupcake holder onto the other end of the needle (Figure 2).

Figure 2

4. Place a clear bowl or pitcher over the needle and cupcake holder. Make sure it is large enough so that it does not touch the cupcake holder.

5. Attach a horseshoe magnet to a piece of string and rotate it above the bowl (Figure 3). Watch what happens to the aluminum cupcake holder.

Figure 3

WHY IT WORKS

The magnetic field from the spinning magnet causes a very weak electric current in the aluminum cupcake holder. This current creates an electromagnetic field which turns the cupcake holder into a temporary magnet. The field pulls the holder around, and it starts to spin.

Place a handful of cereal in a clear plastic bag. Drag a magnet across the outside of the bag. Look closely to see if the magnet has attracted anything to it.

WHY IT WORKS
Most cereals today contain added iron. When you place a magnet near the cereal, very small iron particles are attracted to the magnet. You could try the same experiment with sand, which also contains tiny iron particles.

MAGNETS AND ELECTRICITY IN NATURE

The ancient Greeks and Chinese discovered that some rocks, minerals, and meteorites are natural magnets.

These "lodestones" can attract small pieces of iron, and they always point in the same direction when they are held by a piece of string. Amber is a fossilized resin. It becomes electrically charged when it is rubbed and can attract small bits of straw.

Make a list of all the things you can find that use magnets. Think about whether they use a magnet or an electromagnet. Would they still work if the magnet wasn't there?

Glossary

Atoms

Tiny particles that make up a substance. Atoms in a magnetized material all point in the same direction.

Attraction

An electrical or magnetic force that pulls two or more objects together.

Conductor

A substance through which an electric current can flow. Metals are usually good conductors. Plastic and wood are usually poor conductors.

Electric charge

A substance has electric charge if it is positive or negative. If the substance gains electrons, it becomes more negative. If it loses electrons, it becomes more positive.

Electric forces exist between charged particles.

Electrical circuit

The path that an electric current flows along. It must be an unbroken loop or the electricity will not flow.

Electrical current

A flow of electric charge, often around a circuit. Current flows from the negative terminal of a battery around the circuit and to the positive battery terminal.

Electrical motor

A machine that turns electricity into movement by using a magnet.

Electromagnet

An iron or steel object surrounded by a coil of wire that acts like a magnet when a current flows through the wire.

Electrons

In each atom there are one or more electrons. Each electron carries a negative electrical charge. The flow of electrons is what we call electricity.

Insulator

A substance that cannot conduct electric current at all. Rubber is an insulator.

Magnetic field

The space around a magnet where the magnet has magnetic influence. Magnetic objects in this field are pulled toward the magnet.

Magnetic poles

Areas on a magnet or on the Earth (north and south) where the force of attraction or repulsion is strongest.

Repulsion

Electrical or magnetic forces that are given out by two or more objects. These forces push against each other to drive the objects apart.

Resistance

The ability of a substance to slow down the flow of electric current. Graphite is an example of a resistor.

Solution

A fluid where one substance has dissolved completely in another one.

Static electricity

Electricity that results from friction and does not flow as a current. It can jump from one material to another, as seen in lightning.

Index